Previous Books by Lloyd Schwartz

These People, Wesleyan Poetry Series, Wesleyan University Press, 1981
Elizabeth Bishop and Her Art (editor), University of Michigan Press, 1983
Goodnight, Gracie, Phoenix Poets, University of Chicago Press, 1992
Cairo Traffic, Phoenix Poets, University of Chicago Press, 2000
Lloyd Schwartz: Greatest Hits 1973-2000 (chapbook), Pudding House Publications, 2003
Elizabeth Bishop: Poems, Prose, and Letters (editor), The Library of America, 2008
Elizabeth Bishop, *Prose,* Centennial Edition (editor), Farrar, Straus and Giroux, 2011
Music In—and On—the Air, Arrowsmith Press, 2013
Little Kisses, Phoenix Poets, University of Chicago Press, 2017
Who's on First? New and Selected Poems, Phoenix Poets, University of Chicago Press, 2021
The View from Somerville: An anthology of student poetry (editor), Cervena Barva Press, 2022
He Tells His Mother What He's Working On (Chapbook), Grolier Poetry Press, 2026

ARTUR SCHNABEL AND JOSEPH SZIGETI PLAY MOZART AT THE FRICK COLLECTION (APRIL 4, 1948)

and other poems

ARTUR SCHNABEL AND JOSEPH SZIGETI PLAY MOZART
AT THE FRICK COLLECTION (APRIL 4, 1948)
and other poems

Lloyd Schwartz

© 2026 Lloyd Schwartz
All Rights Reserved

ISBN: 979-8-9904050-8-0

Library of Congress Control Number: 2025927013

Boston — New York — San Francisco — Baghdad
San Juan — Kyiv — Istanbul — Santiago, Chile
Beijing — Paris — London — Cairo — Madrid
Milan — Melbourne — Jerusalem — Darfur

11 Chestnut St.
Medford, MA 02155

arrowsmithpress@gmail.com
www.arrowsmithpress.com

The seventy-third Arrowsmith book was typeset & designed by
Gerard Robertson for Askold Melnyczuk & Alex Johnson in Garamond
Font

ARTUR SCHNABEL AND JOSEPH SZIGETI PLAY MOZART AT THE FRICK COLLECTION (APRIL 4, 1948)

and other poems

by LLOYD SCHWARTZ

ARROWSMITH
PRESS

CONTENTS

13	The Gardener's Song (after Attila József)
15	Lucifer in New York
25	Rubble
28	Angel
32	In Purgatory
34	Lucifer's Labyrinth
39	Sentimental Conversation (after Paul Verlaine)
41	Corona Blues
49	Intimate Visits
51	Officer and Laughing Girl
53	Friendships and Time
55	Unexpected Oracles
65	Fish (after Viktor Neborak)
69	American Treasure (*Show Boat*, 1936)
80	Titian's *Marsyas*
82	Vermeer's Pearl
85	Ralph Hamilton's Faces
89	Lubitsch's *Angel*
93	Artur Schnabel and Joseph Szigeti Play Mozart at the Frick Collection (April 4, 1948*)*

Acknowledgments

The author gratefully acknowledges the editors of the publications in which these poems first appeared.

The Brooklyn Rail: "Artur Schnabel and Joseph Szigeti Play Mozart at the Frick Collection (April 4, 1948)"
Consequence: "Rubble"
The Eloquent Poem: "Titian's *Marsyas*"
From Three Worlds: New Ukrainian Writing: "Fish"
Harvard Review: "Lubitsch's *Angel*" and "Vermeer's Pearl"
Ibbetson Street: "Lucifer's Labyrinth"
Kenyon Review: "Unexpected Oracles"
Lily Poetry Review: "Corona Blues"
Ploughshares: "Friendships and Time," "Angel," and "The Gardener's Song"
Plume: "In Purgatory" and "Sentimental Conversation"
Pratik: "Intimate Visits"
Revel: "American Treasure (*Show Boat*, 1936)"
Salmagundi: "Ralph Hamilton's Faces"
TriQuarterly: "Lucifer in New York"

"Titian's *Marsyas*," "Vermeer's Pearl," "Ralph Hamilton's Faces," and "Lubitsch's *Angel*" were previously included in *Who's on First? New and Selected Poems*, University of Chicago Press, 2021

"Vermeer's Pearl" was selected for *The Best American Poetry 2019* (edited by Major Jackson)

"Lucifer in New York" was reprinted by *Poetry Daily*, July 28, 2004

"Officer and Laughing Girl," as part of the series "Vermeers," won the New England Poetry Club's Daniel Varoujan Prize.

It was subsequently anthologized in *The Sleeve Must Be Illegal & Other Reflections on Art at the Frick*, edited by Michaelyn Mitchell and published by The Frick Collection in association with DelMonico Books, 2020

Viktor Neborak's "Fish" is an adaptation of a translation from the Ukrainian by Virlana Tkacz and Wanda Phipps. It was commissioned by Ed Hogan and Askold Melnyczuk for the anthology *From Three Worlds: New Ukrainian Writing*, Zephyr Press, 1996.

My special thanks to Tara Skurtu for her infallible eye and ear and her consistently illuminating advice. To Frank Bidart for his decades of transformational oversight, most recently vis-à-vis the title poem of this collection and for his generous gift which made this poem possible. To George Kalogeris and the Suffolk University English Department, the Guggenheim Foundation, and the Academy of American Poets. And to Alice Mattison, Bob Ginsberg, Roger Rosenblatt, Gail Mazur, Askold Melnyczuk, and as always, David Stang.

LS

THE GARDENER'S SONG

after Attila József

In a garden of my own making
The trees and I will soon be waking.
Shyly, I'll while away the hours
Planting seeds and tending flowers.

And so I'll sow and so I'll reap,
Planting, planting in my sleep.
So what if all the flowers are weeds?
Don't all of us derive from seeds?

I'll drink my milk, and smoke my pipe
Till even my good name gets ripe.
If danger's lurking all around
I'll plant myself inside the ground.

We need this, need this—East and West—
We know this, know what's for the best.
And if the world's too late to save
I'll plant a flower on its grave.

LUCIFER IN NEW YORK

"What happened there—*now all of you must adjust your brains*—is the greatest work of art ever...."

*

"They were overjoyed when the first plane hit the building, so I said to them: be patient."

*

"Look, Teacher, the birds are on fire."

*

"What do we do? What do we do?"

*

"When people see a strong horse and a weak horse, by nature, they will like the strong horse."

*

"It was raining bodies."

*

"Watching TV—it's like watching pornography; watching ourselves getting fucked by those planes, over and over. And we can't stop, we can't get enough of it."

*

"People running, billows of smoke, shaky cameras—it looked like some cheap disaster movie."

*

"Everyone was whispering."

*

"All they knew was that they have a martyrdom operation."

*

"I really believe that the pagans, and the abortionists, and the feminists, and the gays and the lesbians who are actively trying to make that an alternate lifestyle, the ACLU, People for the American Way—I point the finger in their face and say, 'You helped this happen.'"

*

"Lobbing cruise missiles from 2000 miles away—*that's* cowardly."

*

"We should invade their countries, kill their leaders, and convert them to Christianity."

*

"All Americans need to watch what they say, watch what they do."

*

"In other words, the American flag stands for intimidation, censorship, violence, bigotry, sexism, homophobia and shoving the constitution through a paper shredder?"

*

"There are organizations within the United States that have labored unceasingly to strip religious values from our public square and, in the process, to take away the mantle of divine protection which our nation has enjoyed ever since the days of its founding. However, in no way has any guest on my program suggested that anyone other than the Middle East terrorists were responsible for the tragic events that took place on Tuesday."

*

"DO NOT USE wire service stories which lead with civilian casualties from the US war in Afghanistan. They should be mentioned further down in the story. If the story needs rewriting to play down the civilian casualties, DO IT."

*

"You're either with us or against us."

*

"He's so popular now, he could actually be elected!"

*

"Axis of evil."

*

"Police were acting on information that Mr. Boulez had once said in the 1960s that opera houses should be blown up—comments which placed him on a list of possible terrorist suspects."

*

"There are times when a paranoid control freak is exactly what the situation requires."

*

"It seems inappropriate to perform excerpts from an opera about a terrorist act right now ."

*

"Men are shaving off their beards; thousands of people are lining up at movie theaters in Kabul."

*

"Audiences at the present moment need comfort and solace."

*

"New York City is open for business."

*

"*Saturday Night Live* is one of our great institutions, and that's why it's important for you to do your show tonight."
"Can we be funny?"
"Why start now."

*

"George Llanes's mother unlocked the writer within him with the purchase of a journal during his adolescence. Now those words are all she has left of her only son."

*

"Kathleen Hunt-Casy was a careful friend, who listened and acted on what she heard. If someone mentioned that they had a baby and needed, say, a picture frame, she would find one."

*

"I went mad shopping today, and ninety percent of what I got was for myself."

*

"It can't be said with certainty that Richard Rodriguez was the only Puerto Rican man ever to parade around in a skirt and enjoy it, but his family is certain that no one could have reveled in doing so more than he did. A drummer in the Port Authority's Emerald Society Pipes and Drums, officer Rodriguez was as proud of being a police officer as he was of his Latin heritage. And he didn't mind putting on a kilt and mixing the two. 'He used to say he was breaking barriers,' said his wife Cindy."

*

"At the age of 78, Mary Alice Wahlstrom was a ball of fire."

*

"Officials estimate that as of Thursday, 4,651 people had died, or were missing and presumed dead."

*

"She never wanted to work there."

*

"Who's going to push me on the swings?"

*

"As of 7 pm Tuesday, 5,250 people were killed or still missing."

*

"O beautiful for spacious skies."

*

"It took at least two flight attendants to subdue the 6-foot-4-inch passenger as he struggled to ignite his shoe."

*

"This isn't Disneyland! What are you gaping at? Why don't you go home and let us get back to our lives?"

*

"My mom is down there, whatever is left of her, and I don't want to see some commercial skyscraper built on top of her."

*

"God bless America."

*

"Ya' did good, Rudy, you didn't fuck up."

*

"In times of crisis, we must all decide again and again whom we love."

*

"We may never know why he turned his back on our country and our values."

*

"I still can't sleep. I see those planes in my dreams, crashing into the towers over and over again."

*

"KILL TERRORISTS!"

*

"Officials estimate that as of Friday, 3,187 people had died, or were missing and presumed dead, not including 19 hijackers."

*

"What's the difference between detainees and prisoners?"

*

"City officials estimate that as of Wednesday, 2,992 people had died, or were missing and presumed dead."

*

"This place has to be sanctified."

*

"Tally of dead and missing 2,883."

*

"These dogs are depressed."

*

"She was one of the few hundred actually identified and confirmed dead; and although they only found her foot, she was buried in a casket."

*

"343 fire-fighters."

*

"This is the slaughter of the spy journalist, the Jew Daniel Pearl."

*

"What is coming to America will not, by the will of God, be

less than what has come."

*

"*With us or against us.*"

*

"There is no weakness in reexamining policies that lead to terrorism—we'd be fools not to."

*

"Not for one moment have I thought or felt the way my words are now being interpreted in the press."

*

"I used the designation 'work of art' to mean the work of destruction personified in Lucifer. Of course it was a criminal act because the innocent who had been killed had not been given a choice. . . . But what happened SPIRITUALLY, this jump out of security, out of the self-evident, out of the everyday life—this sometimes happens in art . . . or it is worthless."

*

"All we can do is tell the stories and show the tape."

*

"I pray every day to Michael, but not to Lucifer—that is, I do not allow myself to do that—but he is very present, like in New York at the moment."

*

"Any news from the outside?"

*

"In retrospect, I should have mentioned the national sins without mentioning the organizations and persons by name."

*

"It did happen—right?"

*

"That's so September 10th!"

*

"2,830."

*

"2,823."

*

"The elevators are gone."

RUBBLE

For Mosab Abu Toha

So many books—so many I'd never even opened.

Clearing out my office and the books that had been cramming the shelves for how many years.

How many decades?

Who would want them?

Even libraries were throwing away their books.

Then a colleague friend tells me about a young poet, a "scholar at risk," who is planning to open a library.

In Gaza City.

An English-language library in Gaza!

*

The young scholar arrives with empty cartons—many empty cartons—and a friend waiting in the parking lot.

We start going through my books.

Volumes of fiction and poetry covered with dust.

Shelves upon dusty shelves.

Novels and poems, multi-volume anthologies of English and

American literature.

And writing handbooks.

Who could possibly want those?

But how better, the young scholar asks, for people in Gaza to learn the English language?

He keeps stuffing the empty cartons.

Until all of them are full.

*

I see photos.

The sparkling library.

The new home for my old books—many of them still unopened, still unread.

*

Then the war.

The young poet—our scholar-at-risk—seized from his family, brutally beaten.

His visa confiscated.

His wallet.

And Gaza bombed.

Civilians bombed.

Gaza City turning to rubble.

The English-language library, with so many books still unopened, still to be read.

Rubble.

ANGEL

Did he save them from the Holocaust to profit his soul, or to make a profit?

Did he make them his slaves to protect them from the Holocaust, or to protect his investment?

"He represented the German system—a guy who could make money."

He made them slaves.

He saved them.

He profited.

Was there any other way he could have saved them?

*

Not everyone was saved (not everyone can be saved).

And because not everyone could be saved, the ones who were saved (and their children) were stricken with guilt.

"We the innocent felt guilty what the murderers did to us!"

Some people will do anything to survive.

Who can blame them for wanting to survive?

No day passes when they don't remember—can ever forget—

the ones who were lost.

They feel "responsible."

Guilty.

Why should they (and their children) feel so guilty—do they want this guilt?

Do we secretly want it for them (and for their children)?

Do we need to cast a shadow?

Don't we suffer enough?

*

He was greedy, a womanizer, an adulterer, a drunk—but they questioned only their own morality.

They were slaves in his factory trying to survive a holocaust.

"He provided us with new glasses."

"He delivered our messages."

They called him "Angel."

"We had to accept him as he was.

Nobody else was ready to do as he had done.

He was our Saver!"

*

What did it cost him?

He went to prison (briefly), he risked his life (almost) to keep his slaves.

He kept them even when they couldn't work.

Did he understand what he had done?

When the war was over, they saved him from punishment.

He went to South America, tried to start over, but there was no slave labor, and each new business venture failed.

"... *the thing that destroyed him as a businessman: common decency.*"

He died broken; bankrupt; supported by his former slaves; taking a certain moral satisfaction.

*

In the movie, the wheeler-dealer, the hardnosed businessman "with panache," has a sudden change of heart (like Bogart in *Casablanca*).

He gives up his fortune to keep every slave on his list.

"*The list is an absolute good.*"

*

He turns against the Nazis, sabotages their munitions, breaks down and weeps how little he did, how many more he could have saved.

The movie (quoting the Talmud) says: *"Whoever saves one life saves the world entire."*

The movie makes money.

The director wins an award.

"This never would have gotten started," the director says, accepting his award, *"without a survivor . . . whom he saved.*

I owe him such a debt—all of us owe him such a debt."

IN PURGATORY

Not easy.

Nothing came easy.

Nothing ever came easy.

Everything was hard.

Too hard.

Harder than it had to be.

Everything.

Did everything have to be so hard?

Harder than it had to be?

So much harder?

Everything?

Did anything ever come easy?

Easier?

Can I remember anything—anything easier?

Anything?

Could anyone have wanted it that way?

Who could have wanted it that way?

Look in the mirror.

Did I want it that way?

Did I want everything to be hard?

Harder than it had to be?

Who would want anything to be hard?

Who would want everything to be hard?

Harder than it had to be.

Look in the mirror.

Look!

There's no explanation.

Nothing comes easy.

Harder than it has to be.

Everything.

LUCIFER'S LABYRINTH

Morning Star—that was my name!—*Bringer
of Light*. But since my unfortunate fall they call me

Lice Fur, Life Cur, Rice Flu, and *Uric Elf.
If Ulcer. If Lucre. If Cruel* (oh, cruel *if!*).

Within my name: cruel and cure, fire *(some say
the world will end in fire)* and *(some say)* ice. Relic.

And rue.

What's lying in *your* name?

> *Anarchist Moll
> Bezel This Phobia
> Brisk Entropy*
>
> *Fervid Dray
> Glum Az Air
> Lone Frat Ink Bard*
>
> *Retell or Blow
> Sly Waltz Chord
> Suck Glue Oil*

*

Exiled in Purgatory, divided against myself, what's left except to accept the contradictions

lying in words.

Give me a word—I'll tell you what's inside it.

    Pursuer? *Usurper.*
    Marital? *Martial.*
    Gateway? *Getaway.*

    Editing? *Dieting ignited.*
    Cinema? *Anemic.*
    Gunshot? *Gush not. Hug snot. Hung sot hugs not.*

    Listen? *Silent.*

*

    "The question is," said Alice, "whether you can make words mean so many different things."

    "The question is," said Humpty Dumpty, "which is to be master."

*

Caution conceals action and cant.

Sermons deliver sores and snores.

Victory brings us a City of Ivory, or a City of Rot.

Writings twist wits. Win twin (or tin) wings.
Sing sin. Swig gin. Stir or sting. And swing!

*

Sinister minister. Ink-drinking trickster.
Tender tinker. Risk-taking grifter. Cerebral stinker.

Imposing imposter. Arresting resister.
Hypothetical hipster. Persistent tryster.

Pre-existent exister. Insistent insister.
Replace my transistor. Eclipse my assister.

Burst my blister. Tickle my sister
With the blinking inkling of an oncoming twister.

ASSIST EXIST INSIST PERSIST RESIST

*

Welcome to my labyrinth—can you follow
the thread?

    Eat earth. Eat death. Eat head.
    Dear Death, have you read? Have you heard?

    Teachers cheat cheaters. Cheaters teach teachers.
    Who teaches you? What reaches you?

    A heart aches—do you hear? Do you care?

What's hiding in this labyrinth
    —like an asp in a spa

    or the rat in art?

*

Someplace, I promise, *someplace*—

                  *

YOU HAVE MY WORD—

                  *

my word will be lying.

                  *

My word will be lying.

                  *

I give you my word.

SENTIMENTAL CONVERSATION

after Paul Verlaine

In an ancient park, isolated and icy,
Two passing shapes come passing by.

Their lips are slack, their eyes dead,
It takes effort to make out their words.

In the ancient park, isolated, icy,
Two ghosts trying to call back their past.

—Do you ever think about our old ecstasy?
—Why would you want me to remember that?

—Does your heart still beat faster only at my name?
Do you still see my soul in your dreams? —No.

—Oh! Those lovely days of happiness, unspeakable,
When we seemed joined at the mouth! —Possibly.

—The sky, how blue it was, we had such great hopes!
—Hope has flown off, wounded, through black clouds.

Soon they disappeared through the tangled weeds
And only night understood their words.

CORONA BLUES

> *"Because of Coronavirus, you are going to be quarantined. But you have a choice. Do you (A)— quarantine with your wife and child, or (B)—"*
>
> *"B!"*

*

> *"There is only time for this merciless inventory,"*
>
> Eavan Boland, *"Quarantine"*

I.

It's the night before shutdown, and we're determined to do something heroic.

What were we afraid of?

After all our years together, we decide to get married.

*

First thing in the morning we call City Hall.

We're told to go to the Court House.

It's raining.

The traffic is heavy.

And there's already a line.

When we're finally at the counter, the clerk tells us we'd been misinformed.

We have to apply for our license at City Hall.

On the other side of town.

In the heavy traffic.

In the heavy rain.

At City Hall, we get on another line to get the application we need to get approved at the Court House to get our license at City Hall.

And City Hall, the security guard reminds us, will be closing at noon.

Indefinitely.

*

Back at the Court House, we find two lines.

DIVORCE and PATERNITY.

A guard tells us to pick the line that's shorter.

DIVORCE is shorter than PATERNITY.

The lady at the counter seems happy to see a couple who aren't miserable yet.

She tells us we need to see a judge.

*

In the empty courtroom, the bailiff yells at us to stop whispering.

The judge is nice—she asks us to swear we are who we are and she believes us.

She explains to us the waiting period.

It would be easier to wait.

But we can't wait.

*

The rain keeps getting harder.

Back at City Hall, we need to find a Justice of the Peace.

But the ones who work there are all engaged.

On a list they give us, you find a dimly familiar name.

You like her name.

You phone—and she answers!

"Come on over!" she tells us.

She works right across the street.

She's married people before—and she's good at it.

Her officemates are enthusiastic witnesses.

Everyone's happy.

Then she reminds us we still need to get our license.

She grabs her raincoat, says "Come on!"—and races with us back to City Hall.

She sails into the office: "Hi, girls!"

"Hi, Denise!" they call back.

"Stop everything! These nice folks need a license."

But the printer's down.

"Get Jack!" someone yells.

It's almost noon.

Then Jack appears and slams the printer hard enough to print out our license.

The office quietly returns to its shutdown, and we, with barely a minute to spare—we seem to be married.

II.

We used to eat out every night.

Every night!

I'd ache for a home-cooked meal.

Now home is the only safe place to eat.

So we order our dinners delivered from the same places where we ate out.

But our favorite places are closing.

We have to cook—which is often a source of tension.

Increasingly often.

*

We must avoid the danger zones.

Each of us fearing for the other's safety.

"Bread for days on end drives all real thought from my brain."

*

One morning a neighbor tells me she saw someone talking to their cat.

"I told my dog," she says, "and we both laughed!"

*

It's increasingly hard to concentrate.

I want to be productive, but nothing works.

Nothing new.

I look at things I abandoned.

I worked hard on them.

But I don't know how to fix them.

*

We watch the news, until we can't stand any more.

Then murder mysteries—for the happy endings.

And old movies.

In a Lonely Place, From Here to Eternity, Night of the Living Dead.

"Every disaster movie," someone says on TV, "begins with ignoring a scientist."

Duck Soup.

*

A friend sends us a link to a video—old dancing stars synced to a funk soundtrack—kicking up their heels with such lightness of being!

We watch it over and over—we never want it to end.

*

You get an email from an old friend:

> *Dad was doing fine, determined to live to 100. On his birthday we had a big party and he was alert, happy, chatting, and blowing out candles. There was absolutely nothing wrong with him. Then he got the virus. First I blamed the faceless pandemic. Now I think I'll blame the president.*

The Queen addresses "people of all faiths, and of none"—and tells us we're

> *discovering an opportunity to slow down, pause, and reflect in prayer or meditation… We'll be with our friends again. We'll be with our families again. We will meet again.*

A doctor warns people from New Jersey:

> *Stay home, please God, stay home!*

*

The president gets the virus.

A friend leaves a message: *Is the bastard dead yet?*

We hold our breath.

We don't enjoy our *Schadenfreude*.

Then we do.

*

We know we're lucky to be together.

But tempers flare at the slightest misapprehension.

How can anyone bear the isolation of living alone?

Hard enough to bear the isolation of living together.

If we get the virus, we want to get it together.

*

Eventually, there's a break in the weather.

We meet a friend for a stroll in the open air.

A pastoral walk in a beautiful old cemetery.

People we like are buried there.

A few days later, we put a down payment on a plot.

INTIMATE VISITS

I was lucky—I knew a great poet, and she was kind to me.

The first time we were introduced I told her I loved her poems. "Thank you," she replied, then turned and walked away.

Years later, I thought writing about her could be my rescue. But having come to know the depth of her privacy, I asked her if she would mind. "I'm afraid there's not much to write about," she demurred. I told her to let that be my problem. Then she asked, "But would you finish it?"

Was she being motherly? Fearing disappointment? Or expecting it?

Then she asked if I would like to meet with her—to help if I had any questions.

So I came to her apartment, for exactly one hour at a time. And she would tell me stories. About how hard it had been for her to get published. About what she had written under a pseudonym. Or published anonymously. Or who her poems were really about. Things, she said, she'd never told anyone.

Once I asked if she would explain a certain line. Her answer: "But it's obvious." Her sign that I could never again ask anything directly about her poems.

One day she was expecting the books she had put in storage. Anyone who'd help unpack them, and brush away the insect powder (she had allergies), could keep any of the books she didn't want for herself.

I wanted them all.

(Years after she died, I slid her Modern Library Giant *Freud* off a shelf, and a piece of onion skin—a bookmark?—slipped from between the pages. An intimate note she'd written to her lover in the hospital, whose family had tried to destroy all their letters. *"[Your doctor] doesn't seem to realize the boredom of hospital life for you, when you are not asleep, that is—but* I DO.")

On one of my visits, we were interrupted by her doorbell. An unexpected delivery. We sat together on her couch as she unwrapped the package—a book she was in. She opened it to "her" page: a poem of her own along with one she had chosen by another poet. And on a facing page, a recent photo—a full-page picture.

I told her, not lying, that I thought she looked beautiful—thoughtful and elegant—though her hair was a little wild and her cheeks a little puffy from her medications.

Without a word, she took the book and disappeared.

After how many minutes, she finally returned, and handed me the book, which I then continued to peruse. But as I leafed through the pages, I couldn't find her photo. That page was gone. The photograph was gone. With remarkable precision she had torn it from the book.

OFFICER AND LAUGHING GIRL

"Who is this man? I can barely
make out his face in the window-glare.
A fierce silhouette. The glowing edge
of his floppy, broad-brimmed hat—
the Devil with a halo! His
red jacket on fire. An assault
of maleness; a mystery . . .

Does he see my terror?

—Or is he staring at the map
on the wall behind me? Or out the
open window? His impatient hand
on his hip, even sitting down.
What does he keep staring at? What
makes him stay?"

*

"Why doesn't she just drink her wine
and relax? She looks like she's
about to cry. I can see the tears
welling up. But no—her eye
is clear. Her hands on the table,
around her glass, palms up—ready to take
whatever is given . . .

What do I have to give?

—I could travel past the edge
of the known world, and never find
a pearl worthy of this smile

that sees right through me,
sees my darkness—
yet doesn't cease to smile."

FRIENDSHIPS AND TIME

My new friend is away
for the weekend—the weekend
drags by. I want to know
exactly what he's doing.
Is the convention exciting?
Who are the new people? Is
Atlanta as pretty as they say?
I'm eager to hear all about it.
—What's he doing now?
The weekend drags by.

My best friend has just
left for Europe. I'm snowed under.
There's gossip, and a question
he'll know the answer to;
I think of phoning, then
remember he's away. It can wait.
In the meantime,
I teach, work on an article,
go to a concert. Time flies.

A friend is dead.
Weeks might pass without a word
before one of us called.
Months might pass
without our meeting; and at gatherings
we might talk only in passing.
Still, we loved to talk,
and always looked forward to meeting . . .
Months have passed; one day passes
like the rest.

I'm visiting friends in
a distant city—it's as if
we'd never been apart. My lover
stays home. We miss
each other; but time
seems suspended. My "vacation"
of parties and sightseeing
could go on forever . . .
When I get back, it will seem
as if I'd never been away.

UNEXPECTED ORACLES

> *"What is the answer? [silence] In that case,
> what is the question?"*
> —Gertrude Stein, July 27, 1946

"When I told him, he was like, 'Oh my God!' and I was like, 'Oh my God!'"

*

"After he dug her up and removed her jewelry, we found him cutting her up into little pieces."

*

"My dad works on the Constitution—you know, that boat."

*

"How was Sweden?"
"Adored it! They drove us everywhere—no umbrellas, no boots, no raincoats. When we got home I said, Dear, let's spend that Nobel money on our own limo."

*

"Teaching history was like looking in a mirror and seeing nothing."

*

"Today I felt so good, I tore up my Dead-to-Me list."

*

"At her age, she would have died anyway."

*

"It's a luxury not knowing when you're going to die. I wish I had that luxury."

*

"I define middle age as halfway between my age and death."

*

"That's impossible! I haven't finished being seven yet."

*

"Do you have a good memory or a bad one?"
"Yes."

*

"He told me I was suffering from a mild ridiculopathy."

*

"If you need immediate assistance, press zero."

*

"Nothing has ever happened to me in an elevator."

*

"You were always afraid that a boy might go too far—I was afraid he wouldn't."

*

"If I had married that German count I would have ended up a lampshade."

*

"So invite him—I'll dangle brisket."

*

"I don't mind shrimps—but clams, I can't look at them."

*

"Tea-picking is very difficult work, isn't it?"

*

"I put a thousand dollars in and still have a bad bottom."

*

"I love spending money as if I had any."

*

"The apple doesn't hang far from the tree."

*

"Every time I run into her she treats me like a piranha."

*

"Jesse, in his inimical way, didn't leave a forwarding address."

*

"Why you not be pleased I be translator of you?"

*

"So if they give Pulitzers for criticism, how come Mildred hasn't won one?"

*

"All right, so thank you—*thank you* . . . OK?"

*

"In his sleep he said that the machine gun was in the back seat."

*

"One builds one's own jail."

*

"Please don't be mad at me—I can listen while I'm talking."

*

"My life is too full of unsaid things."

*

"Forgetting is one of the things I do best."

*

"Others have already written what I would like to write."

*

"I saw a great sculpture in London—gorgeous!—it was hanging from a tree."

*

"The ambition of the artist . . . to show the lie of the truth."

*

"The difference is often not great but it is crucial."

*

"Without art, people wouldn't be normal."

*

"Living a normal life is a revolutionary act."

*

"An immaculate home is the sign of a wasted life."

*

"It's astonishing and disheartening to know that things we love will no longer be remembered."

*

"Look, it's a real van Meegeren!"

*

"There's no bum like a pretty good artist."

*

"You should turn that into a poem!"

*

"I'm not Post-Modern."

*

"I'm not afraid of Judy Garland."

*

"I'm too tired to hang up the phone."

*

"Well, I feel more like I do now than I did a while ago."

*

"Hey, that's something you can be fucking proud of your whole fucking miserable life."

*

"Do you believe in forgiveness?"
"I believe only in forgiveness."

*

"Art is the arbitrary successfully posing as the inevitable."

FISH

after Viktor Neborak

cold-blooded things
living out their days
in our bathtub
their long slippery bodies end
in see-through tails
their eyes bulge
just as someday they'll bulge out
from their chopped-off heads

they live on oxygen in the water
separated from my room by one thin wall
by another from the mist, dry leaves,
street, buildings, cars
I live with

water and food? crucial
but light from either sun
or socket may not be so crucial

water and food? crucial
but knowing someday they're all
going to die may not be crucial
unaware as they are of their family connection

to other long slippery bodies

on it goes

bodies quivering on the floor
sharp blows flattening their brains
their insides scooped out
and dumped with their scales into the garbage
then they're poached, or fried, their heads
dropped into the soup

no fish is an island
this involves all of us, all of us
processing plants drip with their cold blood
some of us object in poems,
paintings, documentary films
still they make good eating

even while the fish spirits are watching

AMERICAN TREASURE (*SHOW BOAT*, 1936)

Broadway and Hollywood musicals—quintessential and co-dependent American treasures.

Yet how often does Broadway's best turn into Hollywood's worst?

Tone-deaf miscasting, bloated production numbers, songs—sometimes entire scores—rewritten, replaced, or thrown out.

Directors who didn't know, or didn't know they needed to know, how to balance the realistic and the stylized, a balance that comes so effortlessly—so automatically—on a stage.

Of course, there's always the possibility of an exception.

Show Boat was one of those rare exceptions.

A Hollywood musical as good as its Broadway original.

Maybe even better.

*

December 27, 1927: the American musical theater changes forever.

A new kind of musical, based on an Edna Ferber best-seller, with instantly unforgettable songs by Jerome Kern and Oscar Hammerstein II, opens at New York's Ziegfeld Theatre.

An ambitious multi-generational saga of, as one song puts it, "Life Upon the Wicked Stage"—the singer's mock lament over the theater's failed promise of promiscuous glamour:

> *Wild old men who give you jewels and sables*
> *Only live in Aesop's fables.*

Instead of tap dancers and chorus girls with legs, *Show Boat* gave us racism, alcoholism, compulsive gambling, and broken marriage.

And ran 572 performances.

*

In the film, the show's most beloved performers recreate the roles they played on stage.

Paul Robeson—heroic Othello and the Emperor Jones—is the common stevedore, Joe.

Countless delays and endless schedule conflicts kept him out of the original Broadway cast.

Though the part was written for him.

"Ol' Man River"—American anthem of racial anguish and nature's indifference to human suffering—was written for him.

For his resonant voice.

> *There's a question of whether one who wants to sing and act can have, as a citizen, political opinions.*
>
> *In attacking me, they suggested that when I was abroad, I spoke out against injustices to the Negro people in the United States.*
>
> *I certainly did!*
>
> *I have never separated my work as an artist from my work as a human being.*

In his solo recitals, Robeson turned Joe's Hamlet catch-22 ("tired of living and scared of dying") into a battle-cry: "We must keep fighting until we're dying!"

"*My art,*" Robeson said, "*is always a weapon.*"

The State Department confiscated his passport.

*

He could also play comedy.

For the film, the songwriters give Joe a comic duet with his wife Queenie (Hattie McDaniel):

> *"You don't make money!"*
> *"I know dat, honey."*
> *"I never see none."*
> *"Ain't gonna be none!"*

These two pros teasing each other with so much affection.

*

The other Broadway legend is Helen Morgan—the original Julie La Verne, leading lady of the *Cotton Blossom*.

Until a vindictive pursuer exposes her as Black.

Black enough to make it illegal to share a stage with white performers.

Morgan's fragile, throbbing soprano, always precipitously on the edge of tears, made everything she sang seem autobiography.

Near the end of the film, Morgan gets her most famous number—"Bill"—her hymn to an "ordinary man"—

> *...not the kind that you*
> *would find in a statue.*

Yet the piano introduces us to Bill with Beethoven's most heroic theme:

DA-dumm de-DUMM! De-DA-da DA-da DUMM!

Kern had cut this song from an earlier musical comedy with lyrics by P.G. Wodehouse.

But Hammerstein remembered in it something of Morgan's uncanny ability to be simultaneously tough and tender, "experienced" yet innocent.

It had been waiting for her to sing it.

> *I can't explain, it's surely not his brain*
> *that makes me thrill.*
> *I love him because he's… I don't know—*

Julie sacrifices her own shaky future to give her darling Magnolia—the show-boat captain's desperate daughter, now a single mother—her big break.

Does Julie need to self-destruct?

Did Morgan?

Show Boat was her last film.

In five years, at 41, she'd be dead of cirrhosis.

*

The movie's biggest name (literally the name in the largest type) is Irene Dunne.

Nearly a decade earlier, she played the teen-aged Magnolia in *Show Boat's* first road company.

She was already nearly 30.

Then, in only her second film, an epic Western—aging from frontier girl to wealthy dowager—she got nominated for an Oscar.

She'd star in films with songs Kern had written on Broadway for Morgan.

Co-starring with Fred Astaire and Ginger Rogers in Kern's *Roberta*, she sang with poignantly impeccable diction:

> *Now laughing friends deride*
> *Tears I cannot hide.*

In *Show Boat*, she dances with a goofy abandon triggered by

Morgan singing about love making you helpless:

> *Fish gotta swim, birds gotta fly,*
> *I gotta love one man till I die.*
>
> *Can't help lovin' dat man of mine.*

A "colored" song.

> *"Look at that gal shuffle!"* Robeson chuckles.

Magnolia has just met the smooth-talking gambler Gaylord Ravenal, and that song releases her new sexual awareness.

Dunne gets this.

Her next films—sublime screwball comedies—win her bigger audiences and more nominations.

She'd address the General Assembly, raise money for the March of Dimes, call herself a "Nixon Republican" (then meaning not too far right), play a tender-hearted Norwegian immigrant, and sing what Kern was now writing for her.

She'd be nominated for five Academy Awards and never win, but in her best roles she could make you ache with laughter—and break your heart.

*

The major surprise is *Show Boat*'s director.

James Whale practically re-invented the horror film: *Frankenstein; Bride of Frankenstein* (sequel even more layered than the original); the witty, disorienting *Invisible Man*.

Indelible screen images.

Monsters that move us.

He had never directed a musical.

But he understood "Make Believe."

For *Show Boat*'s first duet, he places the soon-to-be-lovers on different levels—Magnolia on the deck, Ravenal on the dock—"pretending" that their lips "are blending"

in a phantom kiss…

This rhyming "balcony scene" immediately dissolved Dunne's doubts about Whale.

—On Broadway, Morgan memorably sang "Bill" perched on an upright piano.

It became her signature image.

But in the film, Whale just has her stroll over to the piano, plunk down her purse and lean her arm squarely on the lid, and start to sing:

> *I used to dream that I would discover*
> *the perfect lover*
>
> *someday…*

Whale shows us a scrubwoman brushing away tears.

Then he pushes the camera into Morgan's face for the film's most unsparing closeup.

—In "Ol' Man River," Whale begins with Robeson sitting on a dock, leaning back against a splintery piling, whittling.

The piling, clearly an emblem, is bound with rope.

The camera circles Robeson—first from a distance (in awe of him?), then up close (in love with him?).

His face is glowing with light.

Flashback to Joe twisted, half-naked, under the weight of a huge cotton bale.

Wracked with pain.

Icon of suffering.

The suffering center of the film.

But Whale isn't content.

He takes us beyond Joe, beyond the dock, to the wide, glittering Mississippi, rippling indifferently, inexorably into the future.

Then brings us back to Joe, surrounded now by his community of river workers.

And suddenly, as we watch, the pain on Joe's face begins to dissolve—evolve—into a mysterious half-smile.

Resignation? Acceptance?

Unreadable.

Or is it, just for a moment, Whale allowing Joe—or Robeson—to acknowledge the secret pleasure he takes in his own singing?

And the pleasure he gives.

*

Old-fashioned operetta and sophisticated musical comedy.

Human tragedy with an urgent social message still urgent after nearly a century.

Schmaltzy melodrama with a sappy ending.

Conglomeration of irreconcilable cross-purposes, with ravishing melodies.

*

Imagination reveals itself in the balancing and reconciling of opposite or discordant qualities…

Exactly what Coleridge had in mind.

*

Or almost exactly.

TITIAN'S *MARSYAS*

The 16th-century Venetian master's very last painting—as big as life—is the story of the pan-piping satyr who dared to challenge a god.

Titian painted his crucifixion.

He hangs by his ankles from the branches of a tree, his goat-legs askew, as Apollo, kneeling, tenderly skins him alive.

Upside down, his tormented expression reads like a smile.

A thirsty pup is lapping up his blood.

Seated close—rapt—old King Midas, with his golden coronet, contemplates the horrific scene.

It's the 90-year-old artist's self-portrait.

Someone who's learned the cost of making art, the cost of challenging the gods.

And has accepted it.

Except for the glittering crown, most of the surface is rougher, murkier than the master's earlier dazzle.

Close inspection reveals paint smeared by his own fingers.

He put his whole body into this painting.

It was found in his studio after his death.

After how many years could anything still have been left for him to do?

A work is complete, Rembrandt said, if in it the master's intentions have been realized.

VERMEER'S PEARL

I used to boast that I never lived in a city without a Vermeer.

—You do now, a friend pointed out, when the one Vermeer in my city was stolen.

It's still missing.

The museum displays its empty frame.

But there are eight Vermeers in New York, more than any other city—and not so far away.

Sometimes even more.

Once, the visiting Vermeer was one of his most beloved paintings.

It was even more beautiful than I remembered.

A young girl, wearing a turban of blue and yellow silk, is just turning her face to watch you entering the room.

She seems slightly distracted by someone a little off to your right, maybe someone she knows better than you.

Her mouth is slightly open, as if she's just taken a breath and is about to speak.

The light falling on her is reflected not only on her large pearl earring but also in her large shining eyes ("Those are pearls," sings Ariel of a man drowned in a tempest at sea, "that were his eyes").

And on her moist lips.

There's even a little spot of moisture in a corner of her mouth.

Some art historians think this was not intended to be a portrait, just a study of a figure in an exotic costume.

Yet her presence is so palpable, she seems right there in the room with you, radiating unique and individual life.

Already in the museum is another Vermeer in which a woman writing a letter has a similar pearl earring.

She's interrupted by her maid handing a letter to her—is it from the person she's just been writing to?

And in a nearby museum there's a painting of a young woman with piercing eyes and another enormous pearl dangling from her ear (a "teardrop pearl").

She's staring out a window and tuning a lute.

Scholars tell us that these pearls aren't really pearls—no pearl so large has ever come to light.

No oyster could be big enough.

So the famous pearl is probably just glass painted to look like a pearl.

Pearl of no price.

Yet as you look, the illusion of the pearl—the painted pearl, glistening, radiant, fragile, but made real by the light it radiates—becomes before your eyes a metaphor for the girl wearing it.

Or if not the girl, then Vermeer's painting of her.

RALPH HAMILTON'S FACES

> *"...at the end of each century, Boston has had a portrait painter of great interpretive gifts—Copley in the 18th, Sargent in the 19th, and, I'd argue, Hamilton in the 20th.... He is creating one of those invaluable records that tell what a historical period was about."*
>
> David Bonetti, *The Boston Phoenix*

"What the hell is this," Bea Arthur bellowed, when he shoved his camera up against her nose, "an ad for facial hair?"

He always painted his portraits from his own pictures.

Twenty clicks. Thirty clicks. The eventual photos largely unrecognizable.

> *Pierre Boulez. Sarah Caldwell. Jay Cantor. Elliott Carter. Alfred Chandler. Fay Chandler. Phyllis Curtin. Elsa Dorfman. Richard Dyer.*

If he was lucky, he'd find one shot that worked.

Then he'd project that photo onto a 30-by-30-inch museum-board—filling the entire space with the one face.

> *Annie Fischer. Bob Garis. Bob Ginsberg with his eyes closed. Terry Gross. John Harbison. Seamus Heaney. Rachel Jacoff, her face a lunar landscape. Rudy Kikel. Alice Mattison. Michael Mazur. James Merrill.*

Tracing the contours of that face, he'd turn the projection into a kind of topographical map—readable only to him.

Then, very carefully, he'd fill in all the spaces.

He called this his "paint-by-numbers" phase.

> *Alice Methfessel. Mark Morris. Seiji Ozawa. Robert Polito. Anja Silja. Harvey Silverglate. Isaac Silverglate. Craig Smith. Jean Stapleton.*

Once every space was painted in, he'd take a clean brush and start to move the paint!

To brush the paint away.

Turn the board sideways, then upside-down, and keep brushing—brushing and brushing the paint violently away.

"His brushing," one critic wrote, "brings the viewer into direct contact not so much with the illusion of movement as with the inner workings of movement itself."

Stop too soon, the person might not yet have begun to breathe; take too long, the person could get brushed completely away.

High-wire act over an abyss.

Until suddenly that huge face became the face he saw in his head.

Bewildered Klaus Tennstedt. Glamorous Violette Verdy. Michael York.

York, always prepared to be photographed, would "freeze" a split-second ahead of every camera click—and ended up as two separate portraits: each one totally different, each one completely himself.

A hundred faces: Nancy Armstrong to Ben Zander. Comic and tragic masks. Unmasked. The web of our life.

Actors, musicians, writers, dancers, other artists and museum curators.

My father. My mother. John Pijewski's mother.

Himself.

Each face emerging from—emerging from under—that

volatile surface.

"Looking at a Hamilton portrait," a viewer observed, "is like being in the middle of an intimate conversation."

Each blurring brushstroke an increasingly complex disclosure of tenderness or reproof, curiosity or indifference.

No one he particularly needed to speak to; only someone he needed to speak to him.

LUBITSCH'S *ANGEL*

It may be hard to remember, but there was once a time when Hollywood (or some people in Hollywood) could take for granted from the audience a certain level of cultural knowledge.

Art. Literature. Classical music.

Take a film called *Angel*, directed in 1937 by Ernst Lubitsch, much admired for his inimitable "touch"—a film now mostly overlooked.

The glamorous heroine, Marlene Dietrich, is married to a British diplomat (the touchingly stolid Herbert Marshall) who devotes more time to the League of Nations than to his attractive wife.

She loves him, but she's frustrated by how much his desire to save the world has blinded him to his need to save their marriage.

So she slips off to Paris to re-visit a social club where she was once, before her marriage, a particularly social member.

On this impulsive visit, she meets dashing Melvyn Douglas, who instantly falls for her.

Hard.

He thinks she's royalty.

He wants to see her again.

That night!

"9:00 o'clock," she tells him.

"8:30," he pleads.

She shakes her head: "9:00 o'clock."

"But your highness," he protests.

"Oh, by the way," she admits, "I'm not the grand duchess…. quarter to nine."

She never tells him her name.

He calls her "Angel."

Frightened by the intensity of this fling, Dietrich returns to London without saying goodbye.

Still searching for her, Douglas crosses paths with Marshall, with whom, during the war, he shared a "seamstress."

He tells Marshall about his "Angel."

Marshall, though disapproving, invites him home to meet his wife. That night, preparing to attend the opera, Marshall tells Dietrich about meeting Douglas and his friend's irrational infatuation—arousing Dietrich's more than casual interest.

At the opera: Dietrich and Marshall in their box—the camera focusing only on them.

The lights dim.

The opening chords—then fade to black.

Without ever mentioning the title of the opera, Lubitsch assumes we will recognize those familiar chords.

It's Wagner—*Tristan*, in which the trusted young emissary of the Cornish king and the king's bride-to-be fall tragically in love.

It's music's darkest depiction of a love triangle: older man; beautiful wife; dashing young suitor.

Sound familiar?

In the opera, those chords won't be resolved until five hours later, with the death of the lovers, their so-called "Love-Death."

Lubitsch's glancing reference to Wagner is a sardonic yet ominous foreshadowing of the clouds that will in the film increasingly darken our expectation of a happy ending.

He clouds our sense of what a happy ending could be.

And given the surprising emotional depths into which Lubitsch plunges his characters, a happy ending suddenly seems virtually impossible—although knowing Lubitsch we suspect he won't go so far as to end this movie with a "Liebestod."

The amusing contrivances of plot, and the superb acting he elicits from his stars, make Lubitsch a great director.

But he also expected his audience to understand his allusion.

That dark, knowing little joke.

That little quotation—those four famous chords from the prelude to *Tristan*.

They last only a few seconds.

"The Lubitsch touch."

Lacking this knowledge won't ruin the movie.

But doesn't some cultural understanding add a rich—a richer—layer of parallels and alternatives?

Isn't the elaborate care with which Lubitsch sets up and then throws away these few telling seconds the true—maybe even the major—signature of his slippery genius?

ARTUR SCHNABEL AND JOSEPH SZIGETI PLAY MOZART AT THE FRICK COLLECTION (APRIL 4, 1948)

Two of the greatest musicians who ever lived couldn't record together.

They worked for competing companies.

But they admired each other and occasionally played together in public.

One concert took place at the Frick Collection—the most refined museum in New York.

Just outside the concert room hang some of the masterpieces of Western art: Bellini's *Saint Francis*, Rembrandt's *Self-Portrait*, Titians, a Velazquez, three Vermeers…

It seems right.

That concert must have been broadcast on the radio—someone must have recorded it.

I didn't know it existed until a friend surprised me with a copy for my birthday.

One of my most cherished gifts.

The greatest pianist and the greatest violinist of the century—I had never heard them perform together.

I couldn't imagine it.

Schnabel's uncanny delicacy, his sense of tragedy, a trill that suddenly sees into the abyss.

Szigeti's visceral touch, his heartbreaking soulfulness, his "speaking" inflections.

Could they really play together?

If anything, they are more intimately responsive to each other, to each other's odd, individual voice, than almost any other musical collaborators I've ever heard.

Ella and Louie—her heavenly sweetness, his earthy growl.

More immediately—intuitively—responsive to each other than almost any pair of musicians I've ever heard.

*

Mozart's Sonata in E-flat—K. 481, as it's usually referred to—one of the wondrous later pieces he wrote in Vienna.

He was nearly 30—in less than six years he'd be dead.

He was one of the inventors—one of the masters—of the kind of music-making in which the players are equal partners.

Not just a soloist with an accompanist.

Collaborators.

Conspirators.

In K. 481 the players are equals.

Not identical, but equal—a partnership in which both partners can maintain their own personality, their own individuality.

Not identical—but equal.

*

Schnabel begins with an annunciation: three firm notes; then Szigeti puts the period on Schnabel's brief sentence.

Or is it an exclamation point?

Then Schnabel relaxes, almost whistling a little tune (Szigeti gives him room).

Szigeti softens too—their first moment of equal tenderness—not exactly toward each other, but a sudden easy acceptance of the possibility of goodness, of kindness in the world.

They're mutually content.

In accord.

They share their accord.

*

In the slow movement, Schnabel is singing a lullaby—or is it a love duet? (lovers parting?)—and Szigeti is humming along.

Then suddenly it's the violin singing—a quiet lament, Szigeti trying to hide at least some part of his grief, while Schnabel insists—gently insists—on getting past this.

When the opening melody returns, Schnabel incorporates Szigeti's lament, and Szigeti extends his.

Near the end of the movement, the violin suddenly, urgently leaps into another register, another world, as if staying on the earth were just too hard.

In fact, intolerable.

Schnabel's piano flutters in agitation, then resigns itself to allow Szigeti to pour his heart out.

Schnabel lets him, waiting for Szigeti to return to the ground—which he finally, though with some apparent reluctance, does.

And once again they are both part of the same world—where crying out against grief

and accepting it are inseparable.

*

Can there be a happy ending?

Szigeti, maybe reluctantly, seems finally to have passed from—passed *through*—lament, into something close to joy… bringing Schnabel along with him.

Or is this joy exactly where Schnabel was heading from the very beginning?

They are soon not just resigned but happy—equally, if not identically happy—increasingly exuberant, playful, teasing.

Increasingly a couple.

Is that a tear about to fall *(whose?)*—but no, they continue their game.

Yes, they say—yes, we're all right, it's all right.

Mozart says it's all right.

Mozart says "yes."

In a concert at the Frick Collection, in 1948, Artur Schnabel and Joseph Szigeti played Mozart's yes.

About the Author

Author Photo by Spencer Ostrander

Lloyd Schwartz is the Frederick S. Troy Professor of English Emeritus at the University of Massachusetts Boston, the Poet Laureate of Somerville, Massachusetts, and the longtime classical music critic for NPR's *Fresh Air*. His seven books of poetry include *He Tells His Mother What He's Working On* (Grolier Poetry Press), *"Who's on First? New and Selected Poems*, *Little Kisses*, and *Cairo Traffic* (University of Chicago Press). For his poetry, he has been awarded the 2025 David Ferry and Ellen LaForge Poetry Prize, the 2026 New England Poetry Club's Sam Cornish Award, and fellowships in poetry from the Guggenheim Foundation, the NEA, and the Academy of American Poets. A widely-published Elizabeth Bishop scholar, he has edited three Bishop volumes, including the Library of America's *Elizabeth Bishop: Poems, Prose, and Letters*. For his writing on music, he has earned three ASCAP-Deems Taylor Awards and the 1994 Pulitzer Prize for Criticism.

Books by

ARROWSMITH
PRESS

Girls by Oksana Zabuzhko

Bula Matari/Smasher of Rocks by Tom Sleigh

This Carrying Life by Maureen McLane

Cries of Animals Dying by Lawrence Ferlinghetti

Animals in Wartime by Matiop Wal

Divided Mind by George Scialabba

The Jinn by Amira El-Zein

Bergstein
edited by Askold Melnyczuk

Arrow Breaking Apart by Jason Shinder

Beyond Alchemy by Daniel Berrigan

Conscience, Consequence: Reflections on Father Daniel Berrigan
edited by Askold Melnyczuk

Ric's Progress by Donald Hall

Return To The Sea by Etnairis Rivera

The Kingdom of His Will by Catherine Parnell

Eight Notes from the Blue Angel by Marjana Savka

Fifty-Two by Melissa Green

Music In—And On—The Air by Lloyd Schwartz

Magpiety by Melissa Green

Reality Hunger by William Pierce

Soundings: On The Poetry of Melissa Green
edited by Sumita Chakraborty

The Corny Toys by Thomas Sayers Ellis

Black Ops by Martin Edmunds

Museum of Silence by Romeo Oriogun

City of Water by Mitch Manning

Passeggiate by Judith Baumel

Persephone Blues by Oksana Lutsyshyna

The Uncollected Delmore Schwartz
edited by Ben Mazer

The Light Outside by George Kovach

The Blood of San Gennaro by Scott Harney
edited by Megan Marshall

No Sign by Peter Balakian

Firebird by Kythe Heller

The Selected Poems of Oksana Zabuzhko
edited by Askold Melnyczuk

The Age of Waiting by Douglas J. Penick

Manimal Woe by Fanny Howe

Crank Shaped Notes by Thomas Sayers Ellis

The Land of Mild Light by Rafael Cadenas
edited by Nidia Hernández

The Silence of Your Name: The Afterlife of a Suicide by Alexandra Marshall

Flame in a Stable by Martin Edmunds

Mrs. Schmetterling by Robin Davidson

This Costly Season by John Okrent

Thorny by Judith Baumel

The Invisible Borders of Time: Five Female Latin American Poets
edited by Nidia Hernández

Some of You Will Know by David Rivard

The Forbidden Door: The Selected Poetry of Lasse Söderberg
tr. by Lars Gustaf Andersson & Carolyn Forché

Unrevolutionary Times by Houman Harouni

Between Fury & Peace: The Many Arts of Derek Walcott
edited by Askold Melnyczuk

The Burning World by Sherod Santos

Today is a Different War: Poetry of Lyudmyla Khersonska
tr. by Olga Livshin, Andrew Janco, Maya Chhabra, & Lev Fridman

Salvage by Richard Kearney

In the Hour of War: Poetry From Ukraine
edited by Carolyn Forché and Ilya Kaminsky

A Crash Course in Molotov Cocktails: Poetry of Halyna Kruk
tr. by Amelia Glaser and Yuliya Ilchuk

Don't Close Your Eyes by Hanna Melnyczuk

Tiny Extravaganzas by Diane Mehta

Departures from Rilke by Steven Cramer

On the Road to Lviv by Christopher Merrill
tr. into Ukrainian by Nina Murray

Nothing Bad Has Ever Happened
A Bouquet to Victoria Amelina

The Farewell Light by Nidia Hernández

Downfall of the Straight Line by Charles O. Hartman

The God of Freedom by Yulia Musakovska
tr. Olena Jennings and the author

Away Away by Mark Pawlak

The Miró Worm and the Mysteries of Writing by Sven Birkerts

St. Matthew Passion by Gjertrud Schnackenberg

New and Selected Poems by Glyn Maxwell

A Precise Chaos by Jo-Ann Mort

Where Do You Live? by Jennifer Jean

Coming Ashore by Thomas O'Grady

Crimean Fig / Qırım İnciri
edited by Anastasia Levkova, Askold Melnyczuk,
& Nataliya Shpylova-Saeed

Hungry Ghost by Bruce Smith

At the Same Time by Wang Jiaxin
tr. by John Balcom

The Scent of Man by Tadeusz Dąbrowski
tr. by Antonia Lloyd-Jones

World on a String by Gail Mazur

Fire on the Tongue by Patrick Sylvain

ARROWSMITH is named after the late William Arrowsmith, a renowned classics scholar, literary and film critic. General editor of thirty-three volumes of *The Greek Tragedy in New Translations*, he was also a brilliant translator of Eugenio Montale, Cesare Pavese, and others. Arrowsmith, who taught for years in Boston University's University Professors Program, championed not only the classics and the finest in contemporary literature, he was also passionate about the importance of recognizing the translator's role in bringing the original work to life in a new language.

Like the arrowsmith who turns his arrows straight and true, a wise person makes his character straight and true.

— Buddha

www.ingramcontent.com/pod-product-compliance
Lightning Source LLC
LaVergne TN
LVHW041535070526
838199LV00046B/1676